Chuck Bodak with Neil Milbert
BOXING BASICS

Contemporary Books, Inc.
Chicago

Library of Congress Cataloging in Publication Data

Bodak, Chuck.
    Boxing basics.

    Includes index.
    SUMMARY: Outlines the fundamentals of boxing including
psychological preparation, physical conditioning,
offensive and defensive strategies, and ring psychology.
    1. Boxing.   2. Boxing—Psychological aspects.
[1. Boxing]   I. Milbert, Neil F., joint author.
II. Title.
GV1133.B617   1979   796.8'3   79-50983
ISBN 0-8092-7211-3
ISBN 0-8092-7210-5 pbk.

Photographs by Sharon Petty unless otherwise credited

Published by Contemporary Books, Inc.
180 North Michigan Avenue, Chicago, Illinois 60601
Manufactured in the United States of America
Library of Congress Catalog Card Number: 79-50983
International Standard Book Number: 0-8092-7211-3 (cloth)
                                    0-8092-7210-5 (paper)

Published simultaneously in Canada by
Beaverbooks, Ltd.
150 Lesmill Road
Don Mills, Ontario M3B 2T5
Canada

Dedication

I earnestly dedicate this book to my daughters, Vanessa Ann and Mary Lynn, as well as to all youth, in trust that the disciplines and skills inherent in mastering boxing will enrich their lives. I express my warmest appreciation to Muhammad Ali and Harold J. Smith for our continuing and valued associations. My thanks also are extended to John Lira, Harry Wilson, and Jill Koehl for their technical assistance and cooperation.

Vasil "Chuck" Bodak

Contents

Psychological Preparation 1

An exercise of the intellect is the first calisthenic you must perform in your quest to master boxing. You must make up your mind to make boxing an important part of your daily life. This demands an enormous amount of willpower. The food you eat, the number of hours you sleep, your social life, and your way of thinking, all will be affected by your commitment to boxing.

Motivation is mandatory. To stay motivated you should make a mental picture of the rewards that will be yours when you attain your goal. You will earn recognition and respect. You will have a feeling of confidence, a sense of achievement. You will look and feel better.

One of the foremost qualities that boxing develops is the ability to keep calm and poised under pressure. This enables you to take swift and efficient action at the appropriate time: you make a choice and react correctly in a fraction of a second.

Because of the skills you will acquire, boxing itself will become more exciting and satisfying. You will be able to capitalize on your strengths and overcome your weaknesses. Seasoned boxers display a high degree of physical and mental self-control.

Winning is the most exhilarating experience in athletic competition. If you master boxing, you will often enjoy the experience of winning. Positive thinking will become second nature, and its benefits will become apparent in other areas of your life.

There aren't any shortcuts to success. Should you kid yourself into thinking that you can cut corners, you already are on a dead-end street. And, if you decide to coast for a while, you really have shifted into reverse.

Winning is a habit that can be acquired.

Plan your work and work your plan. Set short-range goals to guide you on the way to achieving your long-range objective of mastering boxing. They will give you a daily incentive and keep you from getting discouraged, lazy, or careless. For example, let's assume you have been successful in your first few amateur bouts by using a left jab to set up your best punch—a straight right. But you realize you will be a much better boxer if you develop a left hook. Developing a left hook becomes your short-range goal.

Reaching your destination is a step-by-step process. You study the techniques of boxers who are expert in using the left hook. You set aside a specific amount of shadow-boxing time in front of a mirror to adapt their techniques to your style. After your left hook is fundamentally sound, you add a daily session in front of the heavy bag to the shadow-boxing routine. Then, when you spar with a slower foe, you experiment with the punch in the ring. You study the situations in which the left hook seems to come naturally. You make a mental note of how your sparring partners react.

Finally, you are comfortable delivering the punch against sparring partners. The time has come to use the left hook as a means of scoring points in your matches. When you connect with the left hook in your bouts, you have attained your short-range goal and moved closer to your long-range objective of mastering boxing.

This was only an example. Your coaches

and fellow boxers can help you set up short-range goals that can be attained through a series of steps over a period of weeks and months.

Constantly remind yourself of both long-range and short-range objectives. The body tries to act on the suggestions that it receives from the mind. That's why it's essential for boxing to become an important part of your daily life.

I chuckle when I hear a boxer say he has "made up" for breaking training for a day by doing two or three times as much work the next day. He's kidding himself. First, he has disturbed his concentration. Second, his thinking is all wrong: it's not the length of time that a boxer works that is most important, it's what he accomplishes physically and mentally while he's working. The boxer who tries to cram has a tendency to forget. Not only that, he probably won't get as much as he should out of his next workout because his mind and body will resist the overexertion.

Without proper emotional drive one will never become an outstanding fighter: "There's a chink in Spinks' emotional armor," said Angelo Dundee, trainer of Muhammad Ali, when told of Leon's late-night escapades that were followed by gruelling training sessions prior to their September, 1978, heavyweight title-bout.

Ali, meanwhile, had learned his lesson.

The first time he fought Spinks he was neither emotionally nor physically prepared, and he surrendered his title to the younger and stronger man. Immediately after losing, Ali made up his mind to become the only heavyweight in history to capture the championship on three occasions. Soon he was back in training.

Prior to the defeat, Ali had embarked on crash training programs before his fights. He had rushed everything, and his lack of proper preparation finally caught up with him. Now he knew he had to do it the right way.

Ali realized that the key to victory was outmaneuvering Spinks. Through a slow natural process over a long period of time he readied himself. Day after day, he ran mile after mile. He did more than 8,000 sit-ups. This wasn't a crash program. This was training by the book.

The second time Ali met Spinks it was Leon who was unprepared. He couldn't cope with a man who had solidified his body, strengthened his legs, and stoked his competitive fires to a fierce flame. Ali didn't win the heavyweight title for a third time because of his punching power. He did it because of his willpower.

To master boxing you will have to be motivated, dedicated, and self-assured. In the ring, these traits inspire the body language that is translated into triumphs.

Physical Conditioning

It doesn't matter if you're a sub-novice or a world champion, the soundest advice I can give you is to get in shape and stay in shape. The fight isn't won in the ring so much as it is in the constant training of the body.

On the amateur level, lack of physical fitness probably causes more losses than any other factor. In the pro ranks, getting out of shape is inviting disaster. I've seen boxers of tremendous natural ability take terrible beatings because they were out of shape and couldn't cope with an average boxer in peak condition. The late Green Bay Packers football coach, Vince Lombardi, once said, "Fatigue makes cowards of us all." By being in the best possible condition you minimize the possibility of being overtaken by fatigue during the course of a match.

Unfortunately, there isn't any secret formula for physical fitness. You've got to take good care of your body by maintaining the right eating and drinking habits and getting plenty of rest. All it takes is a little common sense and a lot of willpower.

Getting in shape is a process that involves some self-inflicted suffering. If you go easy on yourself you can't expect to get very much out of your roadwork, exercises, and calisthenics. You have to pay the price, but your investment in time and pain will produce dividends when you put on the gloves and start practicing the fine points of boxing.

Boxing takes more out of you than any other sport. Therefore, your input has to be greater than it was for any of the sports in which you previously participated. It takes a solid foundation to sustain hard knocks and respond with speed, power, and strength.

Before getting down to the specifics—

roadwork, jumping rope, and calisthenics—let's go back to your sleeping, eating, and drinking habits.

Get eight to ten hours of sleep every night—more if you feel you need it. Figuratively speaking, when you sleep your mind recharges its batteries, and your body gets a tune-up. I recommend a nap every day, but I realize this may be very difficult for boxers who are attending school or working. If you can't fit a nap into your schedule, see to it that you set aside a daily quiet time devoted to relaxing and conserving your energy. To derive maximum benefits from your conditioning program you need stamina. Don't waste your energy.

Your diet should be carefully planned to provide you with plenty of energy. There are twenty-two essential nutrients, and they come from four food groups: (1) meat, (2) dairy products, (3) cereal, (4) fruits and vegetables. For the boxer, the emphasis should be on proteins, which come primarily from meat.

I strongly recommend that a boxer exist on two meals a day—breakfast in the morning and dinner at night. You can do without lunch. If you become hungry between these two meals, I suggest that you eat an apple or drink some fruit juice. Never eat just before or just after a workout.

A recommended breakfast is eggs (poached or boiled but not fried), cereal, fresh fruit, toast, and tea with lemon. The evening meal should be your biggest meal, consisting of a main course of lean meat (usually steak but sometimes chicken or lamb), salad, fresh vegetables, a baked potato, and fruit for desert. Again, tea with lemon is the preferred beverage. Tea quenches thirst, replaces fluid, relaxes the body without bloating it, and washes away impurities.

Fried foods have no place on the boxer's menu. Your foods should be broiled, boiled or baked. The taboo list also includes junk foods: potato chips, popcorn, pretzels, pastry, peanuts and cashews, candy, cake, salad dressing, and soda pop. All are bad for aspiring athletes.

Much worse are alcoholic beverages (whiskey, wine, and beer), tobacco (cigarettes and cigars), and drugs and narcotics. Obviously, something potentially hazardous to your health has the power to diminish your reflexes, strength, and stamina.

Your purpose in training is to produce a peak performance when you enter the boxing ring, not to try to repair any abuse you have done to your body. Being in superb physical condition beforehand means you will have a head start when you go to the gymnasium to work on your boxing technique.

Roadwork—simple running—is the most elementary form of conditioning, and it is an exercise you must engage in throughout your boxing career. It strengthens the heart and lungs, stimulates circulation, increases stamina, and eventually provides a reservoir of built-in energy. For the amateur boxer, two or three miles of running every day is enough.

I'm not in favor of boxers running with one another competitively. Running isn't only a physical exercise; it's part of your psychological preparation. You should find the rhythm that best suits you. If you get cramps, slow down to a walk but don't stop. Walk . . . run . . . walk . . . run . . . until you get to the point where you have developed the proper rhythm and you're running without strain or effort.

Boxers living in large cities should do their roadwork in the morning before the air becomes contaminated by auto exhaust and industrial waste fumes. Equally important is staying off concrete and asphalt surfaces. Pounding the pavement puts too much strain on the feet and legs. The ideal place to run is the park.

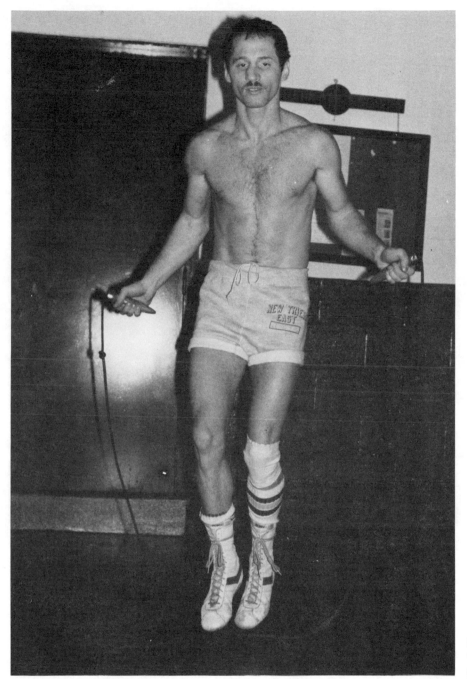

Skipping rope develops footwork, balance, and coordination.

When you get back from roadwork, relax for ten to twenty-five minutes, depending on how you feel and how much you've exerted your body. If you begin the day feeling stress and strain, you've gotten off on the wrong foot.

You can work on acquiring flexibility and muscle tone both at home and in the gymnasium. Skipping rope is an excellent exercise—even if you feel clumsy, for that's a sure sign you lack the coordination that the rope can develop. It's a good investment to buy a rope. If you're in the gym, you won't have to delay your training routine by waiting for others to finish their ropework. And, if you're having trouble mastering the rope, you can do some homework.

In order to learn the rope jumping tech-

Working with the medicine ball hardens the stomach.

nique, run in place slowly, and then begin to spin the rope as you alternate your feet. As your footwork improves, accelerate. You're not only skipping rope, but also developing footwork, balance, and foot-hand coordination. Follow the three-minute-round method of measuring time—three minutes of work followed by one-minute rest intervals.

Stretching exercises such as touching your toes with alternate hands while in standing and sitting positions also can be done at home. These flexibility exercises tone your muscles, guarding them against strains and pulls and enabling them to perform a variety of tasks with ease.

Also essential are the strengthening calisthenics—sit-ups and pushups—that can be done both at home and in the gym. Sit-ups provide the stomach with a protective, muscular shield against body punches, in addition to taking flab off the waistline. Pushups build the shoulders, arms, and wrists. Another valuable at-home exercise is squeezing a small rubber ball to build muscles in your hands and forearms.

In the gym, working with the medicine ball is an excellent means of hardening the stomach. Roll around atop the ball. Let someone drive the ball into your stomach a dozen times. Keep your stomach muscles stiff, and breathe out through the nose when the ball hits. When you get into the ring this "preventive medicine" will serve you in good stead.

Just as with your roadwork, go about your calisthenics in a gradual manner. Remember that you are conditioning your body, and strain is an impediment to conditioning.

I tell my fighters, physical conditioning is a seven-day-a-week routine. Like uranium, exercise has a half-life. The half-life for exercise is two and one-half days. Just to maintain your fitness level, you must reinforce your body with exercise every sixty hours.

There are two reasons that I recommend making physical conditioning a daily routine: (1) it teaches you punctuality and keeps you in the proper psychological frame of mind—conditioning is a natural part of your life; (2) there will be days when unexpected events will make it impossible for you to get to the gym to train. If you are in the habit of giving yourself days off from your physical conditioning program, more than sixty hours may elapse between workout sessions. This will cause you to fall a step behind.

Through physical conditioning you increase the capacity of your body to perform acts that require strength, agility, and endurance. You look good and feel better than ever. A disciplined and superbly conditioned body is the first sign that you're on your way to mastering boxing.

Gymnasium Training

The gymnasium is the boxer's school. Your education in the gym prepares you for the tests that will come during the course of your boxing career. Since your opponents will have varying physical characteristics, styles, strengths, and weaknesses, you must become an outstanding student in the gym in order to excel in your matches. Every round you fight ought to be prefaced by hundreds of hours of training. Every minute counts. Workouts must be carefully planned and well balanced.

Many fighters look forward to going to the gym. Your workouts can be interesting and exhilarating too. A typical training session consists of shadow-boxing, punching the light and heavy bags, sparring, skipping rope, and doing calisthenics. All are of considerable value at all levels of the sport.

Every time a boxer goes to the gym he should go back to the basics. The first thing to do is loosen up. Roll your head and neck, then your shoulders. Bend your waist, moving it forward, backward, and sideways. Rotate your arms in your shoulder sockets, Run in place.

SHADOW-BOXING

Now you're ready to start shadow-boxing, which is a training exercise rather than a loosening-up routine. In shadow-boxing, all that you are hitting is thin air, but there will be times in your bouts when you swing and miss your opponent. If you haven't learned how to pull your arm back properly after missing your target, you can strain a muscle or lurch off guard. Try to shadow-box in front of the mirror so you can detect possible flaws and check out your footwork.

The mirror is the most important piece of

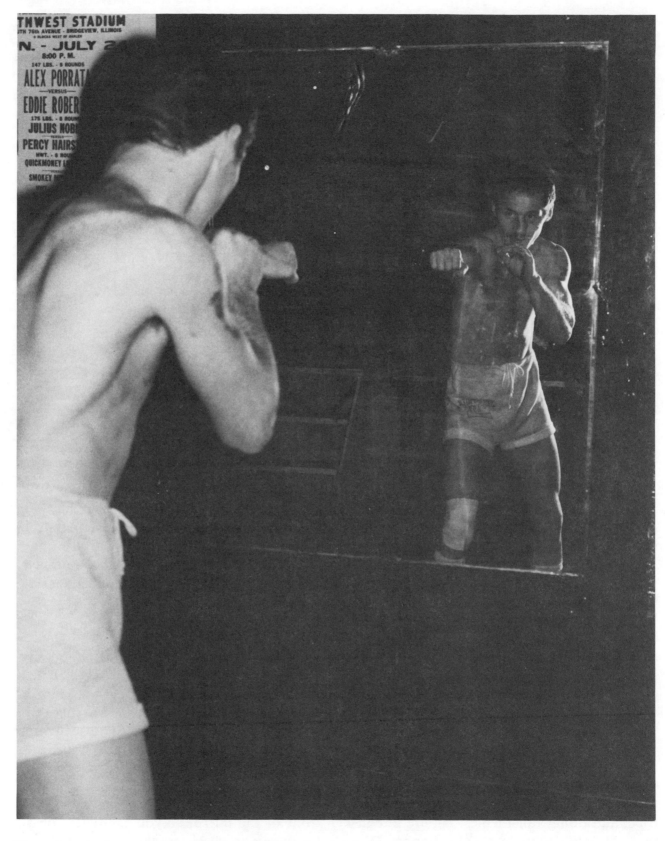

The mirror is the most important piece of equipment in the gym.

equipment in the gym. After you have been instructed in the correct techniques, it enables you to train yourself. You observe and correct the same things that I would if I were watching you. The mirror makes you alert and aware.

In shadow-boxing concentrate on throwing sequences of three to five punches. Work on the combinations that have been giving you difficulty during sparring sessions. Keep moving, pretending an imaginary opponent is ready to retaliate. You want your moves to become reflex actions.

The time schedule for shadow-boxing, like that for all of your exercises, should simulate combat conditions. Shadow-box for a three-minute round, take a one-minute rest break, and resume shadow-boxing for another three minutes.

HEAVY BAG

Using the heavy bag is like shadow-boxing, only now you're landing punches on your imaginary adversary. Utilize all of the movements that you use in boxing. Control the bag at all times instead of letting it control you. When the bag is standing still, move into it. When it moves away, pursue it. Don't shove the bag. Propel it with your punches.

Start with your jab and run out your combinations. Stop the bag with a series of jabs and combinations, just as you would halt the advance of an opponent. Don't work sideways. Your opponent should always be directly in front of you in the ring. Therefore, so should the bag.

Execute, experiment, probe, and test as you box the heavy bag. And always put

Control the heavy bag by propelling it with snappy punches.

snap into your punches. Your training exercises aren't meant to exert you. They are intended to maintain the movements of the body and produce the ability to activate your muscles without strain or exertion.

LIGHT BAG

The light bag is better known as the speed bag because its main purpose is developing hand speed. In addition, it produces hand-eye coordination and strengthens arm and shoulder muscles.

For most boxers, it takes a lot of practice to perfect the snappy rat-a-tat-tat technique on the speed bag. If it doesn't come readily,

attack the bag at half-speed. Eventually, you'll accelerate naturally.

When your punching rhythm is broken and the bag starts to bob, allow it to stop before continuing. Trying to hit a bobbing bag is taking a foolish risk. You could strike the swivel and injure your hand.

Keep your hands up when attacking the speed bag—it's a habit you want to carry over to the ring. Don't forget your footwork. Strive for rhythm and smooth pivots.

In shadow-boxing and working with the speed and heavy bags, it is essential that you make certain your hand and wrist are func-

The speed bag develops hand-eye coordination and strengthens arm and shoulder muscles.

tioning as a unit. The proper way to make a fist is by doubling your fingers into the palm and closing the thumb across all but the little fingers. In this way, the bones and knuckles of your fingers are protected. The shock is absorbed by the knuckles at the base of your fingers. Keep your wrist straight and firm regardless of the type of punch you are throwing.

A boxer doesn't derive his power from the hands and arms. The force comes from shifting the body at the time the blow is delivered—putting your hips into the punch without strain or pressure.

Form is much more important than force.

After form is acquired, efficiency of movement will induce speed. Form and speed combine to produce power. Constant repetition of correct techniques makes form second nature.

Long before you step into the ring to spar, all of the elementary techniques, such as punching properly and maneuvering with rhythm, should be down pat. The objective of everything you do is perfection, relaxation, and control. The great athlete is a relaxed athlete..

Observe, study, and absorb. After you have completed the book, return to this chapter and see how you can apply what

Don't be afraid to spar with a boxer of superior skill and greater experience, even if his name is Muhammad Ali. Elite Studio photo.

you have learned to your gymnasium sessions. For example, when you can execute the fundamentals, you should develop style by working with the heavy bag. Throw a series of jabs, then a right hand and a cross-over right; another series of jabs, then a cross-over hook.

In these exercises you are developing diversity, timing and the ability to manipulate—all of which are essential in advanced competition.

SPARRING

When you spar, you proceed to higher education. Sparring is the laboratory. It is your opportunity to learn like a scientist. You experiment with the material that you have studied during shadow-boxing and work on the heavy and speed bags. You work with your fellow scientists to test for strong and weak points.

Jab and block. Jab and brush. Alternate your moves. By utilizing your strengths and correcting your weaknesses, you acquire confidence and overcome fear. Mind rules matter. Fear is the unknown. Fear is doubt. In boxing you can never separate the brain from the body, and in sparring you discover the unknown and dispel doubt.

Sparring sessions aren't boxing matches.

Spar with fighters from other weight classes to discover your respective strong and weak points.

Never bully an opponent with less skill or experience. But don't be afraid to spar with boxers of superior skill and greater experience. They can expose your flaws, enabling you to correct shortcomings prior to your matches. This higher level of competition often will bring out the best in you.

There's nothing wrong with sparring with a boxer from another weight class, as long as both of you treat the session as a lesson. A heavyweight, for example, can learn to cope with a fast and agile foe by rehearsing against a middleweight. Every chance you get, spar against a lefthander.

In the gym you should get to know your body from A to Z. As a trainer, I can tell you the things I observe. But only you can acquire body feel—the ability to synchronize the movements of the feet, trunk, hands, and head without strain or effort. Then, when contact with an opponent is made in the ring, the body's response is a reflex action.

Although training combines work and study, it can and should be enjoyable. There's nothing wrong with bringing your sense of humor along to the gym. A few laughs are great for both the mind and body. Just don't get carried away. You're in the gym to become a boxer, not a clown.

Technique

Your object in the ring is to control yourself and at the same time control your adversary. You want to hit your opponent without allowing him to hit you. Technique provides the ways and means of reaching your objective. Hands and feet collaborate to furnish protection and striking power. Stance and movement are the most basic fundamentals. Balance is the key to both.

The balanced boxer is better able to thwart his opponent's advances and brush his punches. The effect of the blows that your attacker succeeds in landing is minimized if you retain your balance and reply with a counterattack. On offense, balance helps you to exploit openings and put your weight behind your punches.

STANCE AND FOOTWORK

To get into the proper righthanded stance, place the left foot in front of your body and slightly to the left so that it points directly at your opponent. The right foot is behind you with the toe pointing at a forty-five-degree angle, slightly to the right of your body. The knees are relaxed.

This is nature's way of starting. The feet are flat. In moving, the principle is toe and heel. All of your movements are made by bouncing from your feet and twisting your body.

By landing on your heel very lightly, you relax your joints and muscles naturally. The rhythm flows upward to your joints, hips, and waist. Except when you pivot, the upper part of the body doesn't move. The only movement is a slight bend to the waist.

I am very much against bending, crouching, and bobbing-and-weaving type of movements because they put a boxer in

19

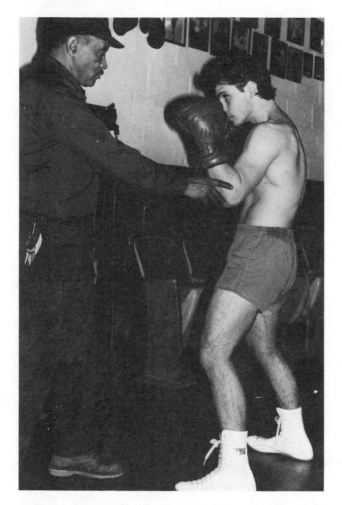

The feet should be flat when in a righthanded stance.

ment—side to side mobility—was the key to our success in Montreal." By shifting your weight you move forward and laterally.

Everything is based on rhythm, which is both a timing mechanism and a method of relaxation. Without relaxation, psychological tension will keep you from performing to the best of your ability. Rhythmic moves are the basis of muscular control.

It's a common misconception that boxers move best on their toes. This is false. You move on the flat of your feet; you *execute* on your toes. This gives you the effect of Move—Set . . . Move—Set . . . Move—Set.

Because of the intricate muscle movements and split-second timing that boxing demands, the Move—Set method is vitally important. It enables you to go from defense to offense, and vice versa, in a fraction of a second.

Move in reference to the position of your feet. When the left foot goes forward, the right foot follows. When the right foot goes backward, the left foot follows. In moving laterally to the left, the left foot moves, then the right. In moving laterally to the right, the right foot leads and the left follows. Your basic position never alters. You merely move in and out of it, shifting from offense to defense and defense to offense.

What about the hands? The hands are alongside the body. The right hand is slightly in front of your shoulder and to the right of your head. The left hand is in front of the left shoulder and completely relaxed. Your arms lightly touch your body. This is very important because it is the basis of my fundamental strategy for both offense and defense—bouncing the arms to and from the body.

Your hands are cupped at all times as if you were holding an egg. (The timing is so precise that you have only a split-second in which to squeeze and lock your punching hand, and supply it with the necessary power.) They are cupped slightly inward to help lock the wrist, one of the weakest joints

unnatural positions and make some parts of his anatomy deadweight. It's ridiculous for a boxer to get so low that he's virtually impossible to hit. You should maintain your leverage. When you assume an abnormal position you cannot box according to the best of your ability.

A good way to see if you're in the right stance is to stand in front of a mirror and check to make certain that your feet are pointing to the left and right. They shouldn't be directly behind one another; if they are, it will hamper your lateral movement.

Lateral movement is very important. In the opinion of Pat Nappi, head coach of the 1976 U.S. Olympic team, "Lateral move-

John Lira, a United States lightweight title-holder and leading contender for the world championship, demonstrates the ideal stance for a righthanded boxer.

By hitting with an open hand, the boxer on the left is risking injury to his thumb and wrist, and the judges will deduct points from his score.

of your body. Thus, when executing a move properly, by flipping your elbow with a snap, your wrist will be protected at the moment of contact with the opponent.

Your head is in an arched position, and the chin is tucked toward your chest and pointed to the left side of the body. When you get hit, the head shouldn't move, fall back, or turn. It's a similar principle to tucking a rifle alongside your head to eliminate the "kick" that comes when a round is fired. In this way you absorb the punch and it travels through the body, lessening the shock. If the head takes the full force of the blow, the nerves will be pinched and the supply of blood will be cut off. This will either make you dazed and groggy, or, if the punch is hard enough, it will knock you out.

I'm a firm believer that you should watch the hands of your opponent. Trying to decipher his intentions by watching his shoulders and feet causes mass confusion. He doesn't hit you with his shoulders and feet: he hits you with his hands.

Although you concentrate on the hands, your field of vision should take in your rival's body from the waist up so that you can immediately attack when an opening appears.

STYLE

Style evolves from technique. Many great fighters, such as Muhammad Ali, have instinctive moves that are completely natural

Watch the hands
of your opponent
. . . . He hits you
with his hands.

for their physical gifts. But I don't recommend that amateurs emulate Muhammad's unconventional technique of keeping his left hand dangling and firing the jab from waist level. Neither do I advocate Floyd Patterson's peek-a-boo style or Ken Norton's unorthodox stance in which he keeps his left down and crosses his right hand in front of his head.

While you shouldn't copy fighters, I encourage you to experiment and try various styles in your sparring session. No matter how intelligent your coach is, you are still the one who must prove yourself in the ring. Many times you will discover that you can add to what you have learned from both your teachers and this instructional guide. I want you to make learning a continuing process. A trainer's work is to educate a fighter, not to dominate him or act as a dictator.

The fundamentals of stance and movement are all-important. Even if you have a knockout punch that lands like a ton of bricks, you need a good, fundamental foundation which will enable you to attain a position to make contact with your opponent, and which will make a positive impact on the judges' scorecards. Moreover, the time will eventually come when you need boxing ability to bail out of trouble.

Many knockout punchers forget about technique when they achieve early success because of their slugging ability. This is the worst mistake they can make. Being obsessed with getting a KO has resulted in countless losses, particularly on the amateur level. The first thing you know, the fight is over and your opponent has outscored you. He has won simply because he was constantly aware of your ability to hit with power and he was always defending himself against it, scoring points in the process.

Remember, the object of boxing isn't to throw punches with the intent of knocking someone out. Strive for perfect relaxation and control. You want to be so relaxed and so much in control that you aren't even aware of which punches you are using to

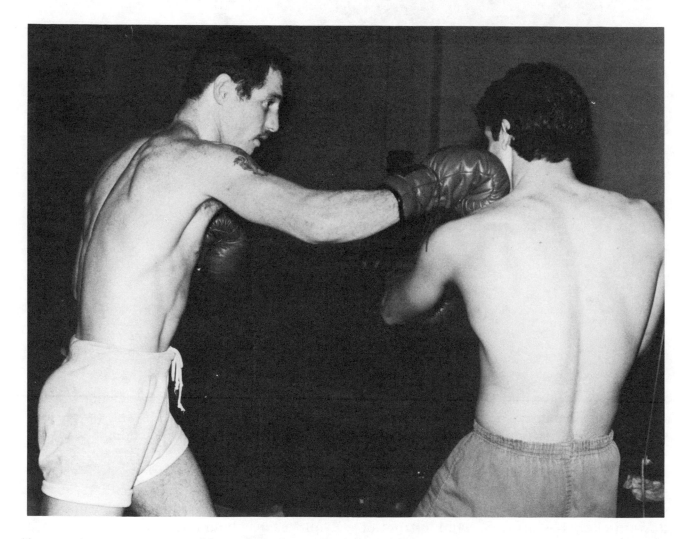

You can increase your punching power by perfecting your technique.

put your opponent out of commission. Your concentration should be riveted on outmaneuvering, outsmarting, and outpunching your opponent, and being razor-sharp on defense. Ideally, you will be able to KO your opponent with any one of your punches, not just with your Sunday punch. And even if you don't have the ability to KO an opponent, you can still master boxing. Some of the greatest fighters who ever lived didn't have that talent; so consider yourself in good company.

Although you may not be able to acquire a knockout punch, you can improve your punching power by perfecting your technique. Form is much more important than force. After form is acquired, efficiency of movement will produce speed. Form and speed combine to produce maximum power. Constant repetition of correct techniques makes form second nature. Always work on eliminating your mistakes. When your trainer points them out, he is doing it to help you.

As a trainer, I'm not concerned with dwelling on what you're doing correctly. You know your good points as well as I do. But I'm constantly going to remind you of what you're doing wrong. If you lose a match, I want your opponent to earn his victory. I never want you to beat yourself by repeatedly making mistakes.

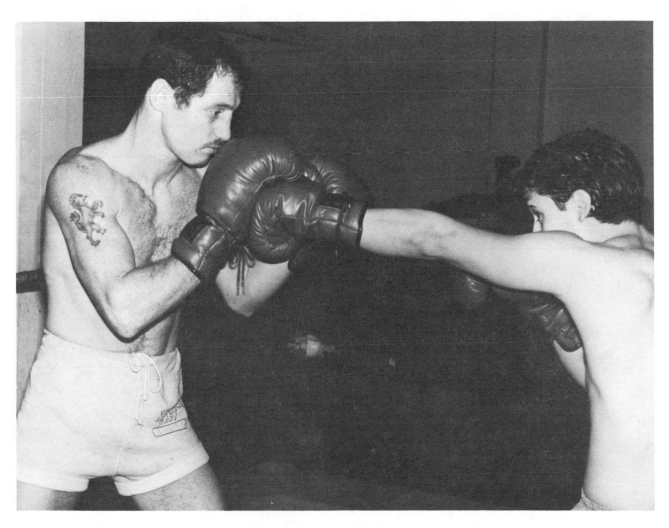

Constant repetition of correct techniques makes fine form second nature.

Offensive Fundamentals

In order to win a boxing match, you must either outpoint your opponent or overpower him. Very few top caliber fighters are armed with a single overpowering weapon, such as Joe Frazier's famous left hook. Therefore, it's essential to have several weapons at your disposal when you mount your attack.

LEFT JAB

For the righthanded boxer, the most important punch is the left jab. By throwing the left jab relentlessly, you force your foe to assume a defensive posture. His response to your jabs also creates openings for the other basic punches: the right cross, the left hook, and the uppercuts with both hands.

The left jab is thrown with the arm fully extended and with a snap so that you feel the thrust all the way to your shoulder. Think of it as throwing and catching a baseball. At the instant of contact you squeeze, just as you do when you catch a ball.

In unison with your fist, the left leg snaps forward, followed by the right leg. At the same time your right hand comes out openly in front of your face to catch your opponent's jab. I call this technique "jab and block."

Every time you jab, expect your opponent to respond with a jab. Even if he doesn't, it's not a wasted motion. Precautionary measures should become habitual, regardless of what a particular opponent is doing. Never take anything for granted. If your opponent jabs back, you catch the punch. If not, you come right back into the ready position.

I can't overemphasize the importance of your hands. They are the same as a cane to a blind man. You cannot execute a move if

Throwing the left jab relentlessly forces your opponent to assume a defensive posture and creates openings for your other punches.

The left jab is thrown with a snap that is felt all the way to the shoulder.

The feel of the left jab making contact tells you when to move again and where to move. *Chicago Tribune* photo.

you cannot feel. That's the principle of the jab. It makes contact and, in the process, tells you when to move again and where to move. It is the key to your subsequent combinations.

You throw your left jab with the palm down and with a pushing and pressing technique. The trajectory depends on the height of your opponent: If you're shorter than your foe you'll be punching upward; if you're taller, you'll be punching downward. Regardless, the fundamentals are the same.

The arm is fully extended with a snap; you move into your opponent; you use a pushing and pressing technique; you feel for openings; and you expect a response.

LEFT HOOK

When you use the left hook, the palm is in a different position: it faces you. Think of pulling the opponent toward you. The punch is called the hook because you're *hooking* the other boxer.

Because your palm is facing you, your left

The left hook is a powerful punch, capable of doing sudden damage to the head or body. *Chicago Tribune* photo.

hand is protected. Your thumb is a weak digit. If you try to throw a hook with your palm down, the way you would a left jab, you run the risk of injuring your thumb. You also will probably misjudge your point of contact if your opponent moves.

The left hook is a powerful punch, capable of doing sudden damage to the head or body. Your fist, elbow, and shoulder should all be on line as you make a snappy pivot to put your body's power into the blow. Tuck your left arm close to your body, and twist your left hip and shoulder to the right.

Again, expect your opponent to respond, and the instant the punch connects have your right hand in the ready position. Don't telegraph the left hook or you'll be asking for a shot to the head. Don't take a round-house swing, because your opponent will either slip or catch the punch and seize the

A snappy pivot puts the body's power into the left hook.

chance to counterpunch. An experienced foe will have you on the canvas if you fail to use your head when you hook.

RIGHT CROSS

Righthanders should never forget that their right hand is primarily a defensive tool. It does eighty percent of the defensive work: parrying, catching punches, and brushing. But the right can also become a powerful offensive weapon: a right cross can alter or end a match in an instant. The left jab and right cross add up to the old one-two punch—a combination that's still as good as gold. As with the jab, the palm is down for the right cross. In this instance, also, the

The right hand does eighty percent of the defensive work. One of its tasks is brushing punches.

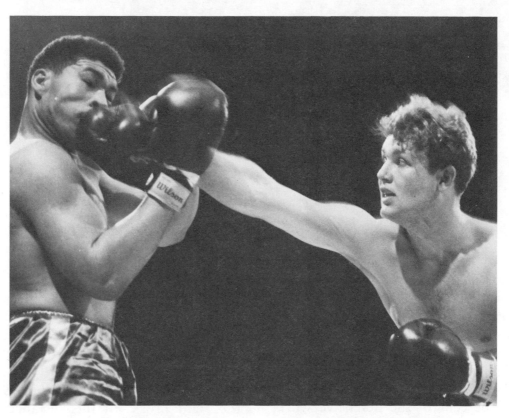

Launch the right cross with a fast elbow flip that puts the fist directly on target. Completely relax until the moment of contact; then squeeze. *Chicago Tribune* photo.

For the right cross, note the toe-and-heel technique, the full extension of the arm, and the palm facing downward at the instant of contact. Illustration by Jill Koehl.

push and press principle of extension applies.

Remember to always keep your right arm in constant touch with your own body. This will enable you to launch the right with the fast elbow flip that puts the fist directly on target.

Shift your weight to your right leg, and let the entire right side of your body go into the punch, applying the force. Completely relax until the split-second of contact. Then squeeze. Instantly return the right to its defensive position, touching your arm to your body.

Unless your opponent is stunned and covering up, the head should be the target of the right cross. Aiming at the body under normal circumstances is foolhardy because it enables his left jab to go over your right and sets you up for a dose of your own medicine.

The head should be the target of the right cross. Aiming at the body enables your adversary's left jab to go over your right.

The uppercut can be used against head or body and can be thrown with either hand.

Below, the uppercut often enables you to penetrate your opponent's defense without creating an opening for a counterpunch. After the uppercut, instantly return the right arm to its defensive position, touching the side of the body.

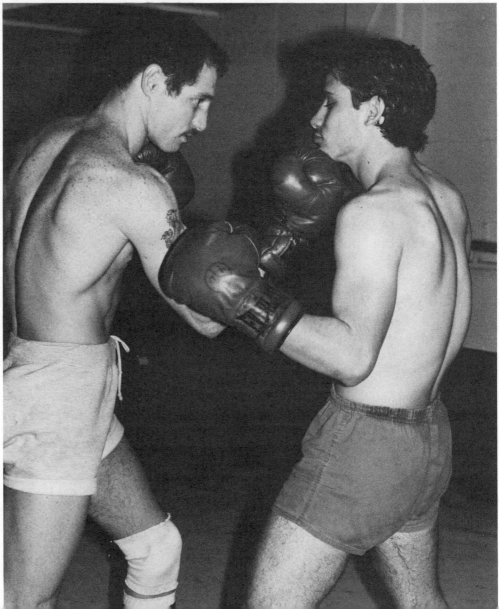

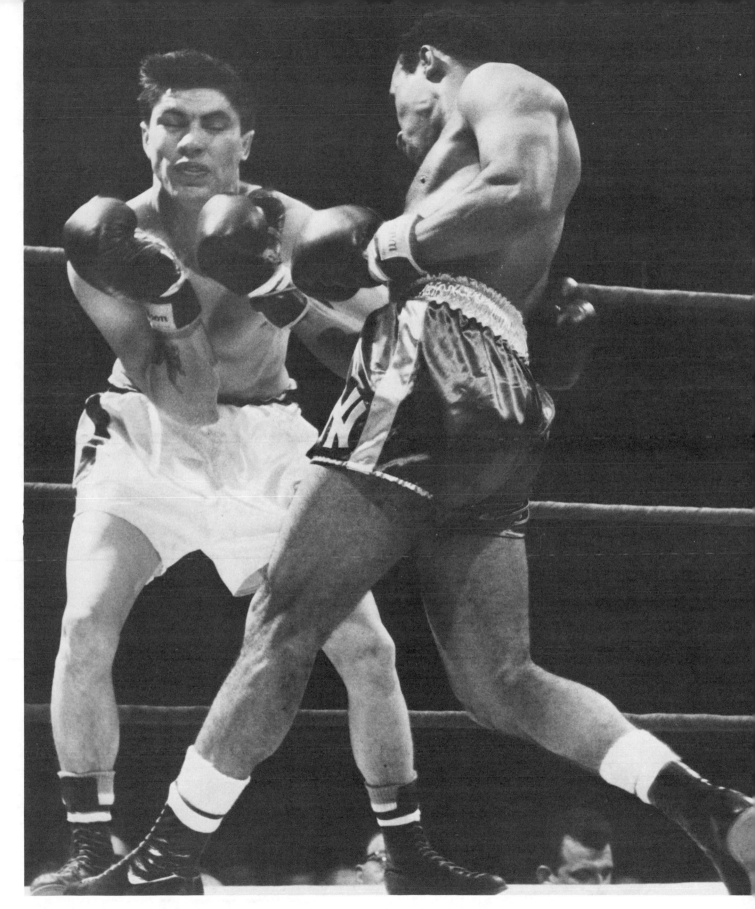

When you fire the right uppercut, the power flows upward from your right foot. Drop your arm, bringing the fist below the target. Then shoot it upward as you pivot. *Chicago Tribune* photo.

RIGHT HOOK

A variation of the right cross is the right hook. The palm faces inward when you hook with the right hand. The motion is identical to that of the left hook, and either the head or the body is fair game. The pivot will produce the power.

UPPERCUTS

The uppercut (like the hook) is effective as both a head and body blow. Both with the right and left uppercut, the palm faces up.

In throwing the uppercut, the principle is the same as that of lifting. Drop your arm, bringing the fist below the target. Then shoot it upward and pivot to generate the body power which gives your blow its force. If it's a left uppercut your weight shifts to your left foot; if it's a right uppercut, vice versa.

The uppercut is very effective for infighting because it enables you to penetrate your opponent's defense without creating an opening for a counterpunch.

No matter what punch you are throwing, make it a rhythmic move. This enables you to instantly shift from one move to another, or go from offense to defense.

These punches can be executed in many combinations. A well-coached boxer has the ability to execute, manipulate, invent, and experiment because of his basic training in the fundamentals.

In my opinion, speed in boxing is just as overrated as the ability to throw a knockout punch. A directed attack is much more effective than a furious attack. You have no control over sheer speed. Perfected timing rather than speed is the secret of success on offense.

A reminder: on offense, always be conscious of your opponent's capabilities. Become careless and you can lose a fight in a flash.

Defensive Fundamentals 6

Boxing is often referred to as "the manly art of self-defense." This definition puts into perspective the importance of defense in mastering the sport. No matter how much slugging power you possess, as you rise to higher levels of competition you will discover it isn't enough. In the early stages of amateur boxing tournaments, such as the Golden Gloves, there are many knockouts. But most championship bouts are won on decisions.

Superior defensive skill is the most conspicuous characteristic of four of the world champion heavyweights: Muhammad Ali, Gene Tunney, Jack Johnson, and Jim Corbett. Sonny Liston was one of the most awesome sluggers of his era; yet he deteriorated into a groping hulk in his two title fights with Ali. Failure to learn the fundamentals of defense means running the risk of being injured. Your knockout punch won't undo the damage after you have been cut to ribbons or suffered a concussion.

This is not to suggest that you should become obsessed with protecting yourself. Getting punched is an integral part of the sport of boxing. But the most powerful deterrent to your opponent is your ability to retaliate. The boxer who runs without hitting is on the road to defeat.

In amateur boxing, when points are equal the decision goes to the boxer displaying the best "generalship"—the development of natural advantages, coupled with intuition, and the ability to grasp quickly the advantages of any opening given by an opponent. "Gen-

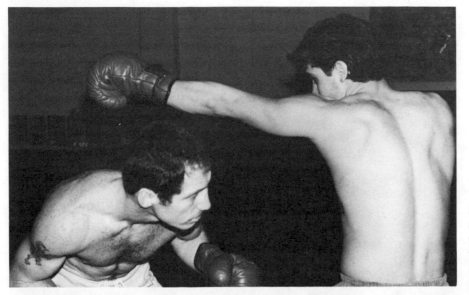

Slipping a punch gets you out of the way but leaves you within striking distance to capitalize on any openings that present themselves.

Slip a right cross by bending to your left without moving your feet. *Chicago Tribune* photo.

eralship" is another name for control. You gain control through timing.

My theory of boxing demands that you always work your way back into the basic defensive position. Defense includes moving, slipping, catching, brushing, blocking, rolling, and feinting.

Moving is nothing more than the basic footwork that I described in Chapter 4—maneuvering forward and backward, and from side to side. You bounce from the feet with toe and heel rhythm. Move—Set . . . Move—Set . . . Move—Set.

My cardinal rule in moving to and from an opponent is based on the fact that the shortest distance between two points is a straight line. It's the fastest and best way to reach your destination.

Move forward, then laterally, Move backward, then laterally. Many times a boxer will make a lateral move as he tries to get away from his opponent. However, he's still within striking range. That wouldn't have been the case if he had moved backward.

Slide in and out, slipping punches en route. When you slip a punch you get out of its way, but your feet don't move, which leaves your body within striking distance and permits you to capitalize on the openings that present themselves.

Never bend your head. Slip by bending at your waist to the left or right, depending on where the punch is coming from. When your opponent throws a left, bend to the right. If it's a right, bend to the left. The instant the blow goes by, counterpunch.

I'm very much against bobbing and weaving tactics because I believe they waste precious seconds. On the other hand, I'm in favor of a boxer developing unique techniques of slipping, feinting, sliding, and moving laterally. Your first priority is to make the fastest and most effective move possible and snap back into the basic position. You want to do more than make your opponent miss; the idea is to hit him before he recovers.

BLOCKING

It's much better to slip a punch than to catch the blow. If a punch sails past or around you, the other boxer has exerted himself; while you have used very little effort. But when you catch or block a punch it causes tension and the expenditure of energy on your part.

Nevertheless, often you have no alternative but to catch a punch. In catching punches, step to the side, turn your body, and use your hands to disarm the force.

Don't use both hands to block punches. Using two hands leaves more of your body unguarded and rules out the possibility of counterpunching.

Left Jab

The technique in blocking a high left jab calls for you to extend your left arm to the side and brush the blow to the outside. If the punch is to the body, brush it down and away.

Should your opponent be a sloppy puncher you may be able to counter more effectively by blocking his jab with your right arm and elbow, and left shoulder. Putting the hands in position is the key. When you're in the basic position your right arm and elbow will guard against left hands to the ribs, and your left shoulder will be a buffer against shots aimed at your chin.

Anticipate. Throw counter combinations and work your way back into the basic position. Set the man up and beat him to the punch. Use the element of surprise to keep him off balance.

Right Cross

The way to deal with a right cross aimed for the head is to extend your right arm to the side and shove the punch to the outside.

If your opponent is a sloppy puncher you should be able to counter effectively.

You can counter after blocking punches with your arms and elbows.

Left Hook

To deflect the left hook, your arm is parallel to your body with your elbow close in. When you see the hook coming, extend the arm and apply tension. Catch the punch on the back of your right hand.

In this instance, an excellent counter (which for some inexplicable reason is seldom taught) is to catch the hook with the right hand and immediately come off the catch with a hook of your own. The element of surprise in your brush and right hook to the head is tremendous, and can almost always be followed by a sharp left jab. The transition from defense to offense is instantaneous and rhythmic.

Uppercuts

Against both the left and right uppercuts you use your right hand and forearm. You keep your left arm free to initiate an attack. Always remember, your left is your primary offensive weapon and your right does eighty percent of the work on defense.

Other than in abnormal situations when you're under extreme pressure, the left is probing for an avenue of attack. Regardless of whether you're slipping, catching, or brushing, the left should be free to trigger an offensive attack.

Set your opponent up with your jab. If he jabs back, slip to the right, bending slightly at the waist, and cut loose with a left hook

When you slip a right by bending to the left, counter with your right hand over your opponent's left.

This is poor form. Keep your hands high or your entire defense will crumble.

to the body, followed by a left hook to the head, and a left jab to the head. Another effective counterattack calls for a right to his body, a left hook to the head, a right to the head, and a left jab.

When you slip a right by bending to the left, counter with your right hand over his left. Come back with a left hook to the body, a left hook to the head, a right cross to the head, and finish with a left jab that puts you back in the basic position.

Now I will review some important points:

—Never slip punches by bending your head. It takes you off balance and puts you in jeopardy.

—When you are hit in the head, it shouldn't move, fall back, or turn. You should absorb the punch and let it travel through your body, dissipating its power.

—By constantly going back to the basic defensive position you minimize the danger of getting devastated by one punch.

—Keep your hands high even though they are becoming weary from serving as your shield. Should you give in to the temptation to let your hands dip a little bit, your entire defense is likely to crumble.

—Relax . . . relax . . . relax. . . . I can't stress this enough. Other than lack of conditioning, one of the main reasons boxers become arm weary is because of the tension they bring on themselves.

Escape and Evasion

Because of the nature of the sport, every boxer must be psychologically and physically prepared to encounter times of extreme adversity. Situations will arise when your opponent batters through your defenses and you are temporarily unable to protect yourself in the customary manner or launch an immediate counterattack.

When you find yourself in trouble you should immediately try to do two things: (1) minimize the damage your opponent is inflicting; and (2) resort to time-killing tactics. The one thing in the world you don't want to do is throw caution to the wind and try to land a lucky punch.

There is a tiny loophole in this rule. Gamble if time is running out in the final round and you know you are hopelessly behind on points. Try to land your most powerful punch when the slightest opening presents

itself. Minimize defense because you have nothing to lose. Everything should be based on offense.

Normally, however, your top priority is making it through the round and making your opponent live to regret all of that energy he expended in trying to put you out of commission.

Sometimes he will become overconfident in the next round, enabling you to exploit his recklessness. On other occasions, some of his self-confidence will seep away when he sees that you have survived his best shots. And it isn't uncommon for a boxer to run out of gas after going on an all-out offensive.

Moments of great adversity demand extreme concentration, control, and patience. Defense takes precedence over offense. Pick your shots like a sniper running low on

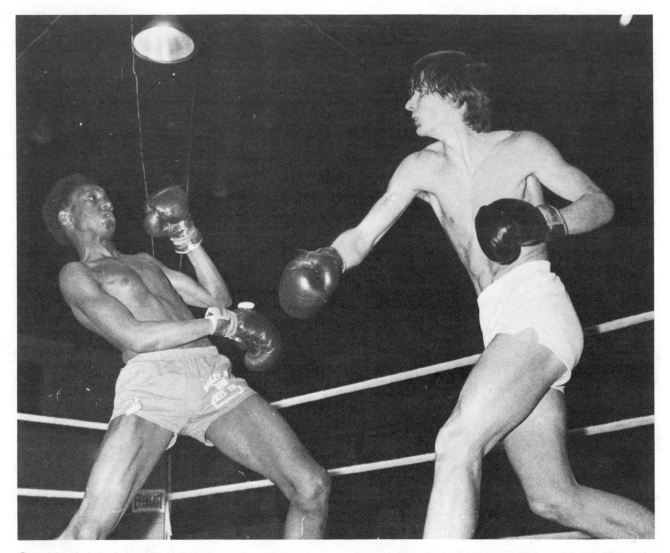

Gamble if time is running out and you know you are hopelessly behind on points: try to land your most powerful punch. *Chicago Tribune* photo.

ammunition. Wait for your opponent to get arm-weary, overconfident, sloppy, and ineffective.

Move—Set . . . Move—Set . . . Move—Set. Maintain your composure and fall back on your basic training techniques. I don't advocate clinching. I think it's a poor defense mechanism. By clinching you exert three or four times as much energy as you do by moving and blocking and at a time when you can least afford it. The only time you should clinch is when you're really hurt

and you're too groggy to assume your basic position.

If you must clinch, grab your opponent's right arm at the elbow with your left hand, and move quickly toward him, working his arm under your left armpit. Apply the same technique on the other side. As soon as your grogginess has worn off or when the referee shouts "Break!" step backward, pushing your opponent away from you.

Assume your basic position. Jab, block, brush, and move. Keep it up. Work from side to side. Resist the temptation to clinch. Don't panic and let the bout deteriorate into a brawl. In amateur boxing, points are deducted for hitting in a clinch, for hitting while holding an opponent, and for failing to take one full step back when the referee gives the command to break.

Relax. I cannot repeat that word too often. The ability to relax is perhaps the most important attribute of a good boxer. Strain, tension, and anxiety take a tremendous toll on you physically and mentally. When you're relaxed, rhythm comes naturally, and rhythm is the key to your safest defensive strategy: Move—Set . . . Move—Set . . . Move—Set. Block your opponent's punches and move out with your jabs.

Often a series of feints and jabs will be your salvation. Anticipate your adversary's aggressive action. Keep him occupied so that he deviates from the pressure he's exerting.

Boxing is a contact sport, and sometimes you're going to get hit. As a rule, you respond to your opponent's all-out attack by slipping, catching, blocking, and brushing.

The clinch is a last-resort defensive tactic. It can keep you from losing but it can never make you a winner.

Situations will arise where you are temporarily unable to protect yourself. Maintain your composure and don't let the bout deteriorate into a brawl. *Chicago Tribune* photo.

Style and Execution

8

When Muhammad Ali lost some of his skills, he could still win with his head. And I can win now by knowing how to win.

Golfer, Jack Nicklaus

Yes, winning is a habit that can be acquired. You must remember that weapons alone never won a war. It is the way in which they are deployed by the generals that determines their effectiveness.

Learning the offensive and defensive fundamentals is a necessity for a boxer, but it isn't the same as mastering boxing. Rather, it is a means to an end. Correct form in the ring can be the proverbial poetry in motion, but inevitably there will come a time when circumstances demand improvisation, and landing punches will become the name of the game.

One of the basic principles of art, "form follows function," also applies to boxing. In this case, style follows execution. Forget about the fancy flourishes, exaggerated movements, and pretty-boy routines. Think about winning!

Mechanical skill will carry a boxer only so far. Beyond a certain point, mechanical skill, even when backed by proper physical condition, isn't enough to win. Winning becomes a matter of possessing the will to win.

The successful person is one who is confident of his ability to continue to achieve. Positive thinking is a source of his power. To condition himself psychologically, a boxer must acquire a positive attitude. There are many instances of competitors who lack many of the physical attributes of great boxers, but who have become consis-

If you're facing a taller foe, slip his left jab and counter with a left jab of your own. *Chicago Tribune* photo.

tent winners through work and willpower.

In his bouts, the boxer harvests the fruits that he has planted by roadwork and physical conditioning, and cultivated in his gymnasium workouts. The match is won or lost by the composite of physical condition, courage, intelligence, experience, and physical equipment that the boxer carries into the ring. If your sum total is greater than that of your adversary, undoubtedly you will win. If it's less, you no doubt will lose.

You box with your head and heart as well as with your hands and feet. A successful boxer consistently outthinks, outmaneuvers, and outworks his opponents.

Begin by taking inventory of your physical equipment. You must adopt a style that makes execution easy. Take into account your build, foot and hand speed, and slugging ability. For example, tall fighters can maximize their advantage in inches by jabbing incessantly. If you're a short boxer I urge you to perfect the technique of working off your opponent's jab. Let his contact provide the impetus for your countermoves. Eliminate the efficiency of his height by getting inside. Jab and block. Jab and feint. Jab and brush.

COUNTERPUNCHING

Counterpunching is an offensive maneuver but it demands defensive dexterity. Before launching a counterpunch it is essential that you have stopped or avoided your opponent's blow.

Left Jab

There are several ways to counter a left jab. Here are a few:

—Parry the jab and counter with a right to the head.

—Parry the jab, slide to your left and throw a left hook to the head or body.

—Slip the jab. As the punch goes over your shoulder attack your rival's body with a left hook followed by a straight right to

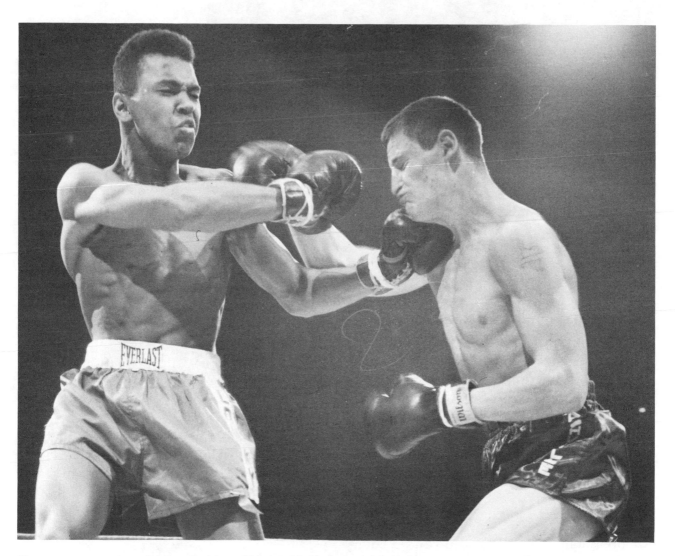

Even as an amateur in the Golden Gloves, Muhammad Ali (*left*) was an outstanding counterpuncher. *Chicago Tribune* photo.

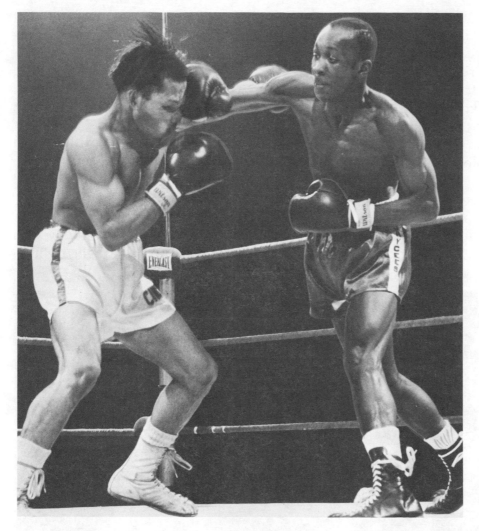

After you block a left hook with your right arm, a straight right to the head is an excellent response. *Chicago Tribune* photo.

the jaw, another left hook to the body, a hook to the head, a right to the head, and finally a left jab to the head.

—Step to your right to avoid the jab and deliver a straight right over the outstretched shoulder to your opponent's jaw, or step to the right and attack his body with an uppercut.

These are basic counter moves. Though short boxers should specialize in counterpunching, they are strategically sound for all fighters.

Left Hook

An opponent's left hook also can be countered in various ways:

—Block the blow with your right arm and slam a straight right to the chin, or counter with a left hook to the head.

—Brush the hook, pivot, and launch your own left hook.

—Slip the hook, throw a left hook to the body, and follow with a right to the head.

Straight Right

For a straight right you can catch the blow with your right hand and reply with a straight right to the chin or head, or left hook to the body.

If you slip a straight right, the ideal response is a left hook or right uppercut.

Uppercuts

To counter a left uppercut, block the blow

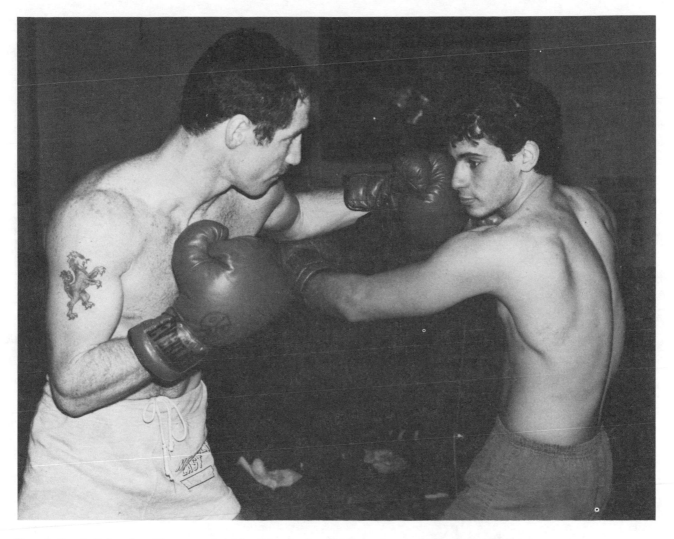

Brush the left hook with your right hand, pivot, and launch your own left hook.

with your right forearm and fire a left hook to the head. If it's a right uppercut, a left hook to the head or a right uppercut to the unprotected midsection will be the logical answer.

If you have a powerful punch, a good tactic is to let your opponent try to mount an early offensive. He may become overconfident and draw back his shoulder, hoping to put a little extra into a right cross or left hook. Beat him to the punch.

The slugger does not need to absorb several direct hits as he searches for an opening to make his knockout punch; just as easily the KO can be the result of a well-timed counterpunch.

In sizing up your foe it's a good idea to jab and block and brush to probe for information. How much energy is he exerting? Does he hit with power? Is he lunging or reaching? Does he bring his hand back to the on-guard position? If he is off balance you can set him up for a prolonged counterattack.

As you progress to higher levels of competition, you'll find your foes making fewer and fewer mistakes.

A feint is a pretended attack meant to lure an opponent off guard.

FEINTING

It will benefit you greatly to become skilled in feinting. When you feint you try to lure your opponent off guard by pretending to attack. If he falls for the decoy, he will be a sitting duck for your rapid-fire punches.

Feints are extremely intricate. When they don't draw a punch, always come back with a jab so you aren't wasting motion. A typical feint is to start a left jab to your opponent's body. If he drops his right glove and forearm in defense, either snap back the jab and turn it into a left hook to the head, or hammer the head with a straight right.

Move your head a few inches forward in a feint and you'll be inviting a jab. If it comes, slip and counter.

Many times when you're feinting you'll have the opportunity to lead with straight right hands or left hooks, using them in place of the jab.

When your feints prompt an opponent to throw a right hand, either catch his punch and hook, or slip his blow and uppercut.

The slugger in pursuit of a fancy boxer should try to cut the ring in half, containing the speedster in one half of the ring by moving from side to side. By doing that you're denying him an escape route when you seize the offensive initiative. A swifty in round one often turns into a slowpoke by round three —after his speed has been drained away by tension and persistent punches to the body.

Infighting offers the best route to the body. Be set to work inside your opponent's swings at the first opportunity. Push his arms away from the body and hit it with close-in punches. Keep slipping and moving side to side, trying to keep him from clinching.

When you get almost on top of your opponent, and he is trying to clinch, rest your head on his chest and keep hitting his body with snappy punches. Maintain your own weight. Just touch his body so that your punches can be effective.

To defend against a smaller rival attacking on the inside, block his punches and move away to long range. If you grab him

you stand a chance of getting battered and having your strength sapped. The object is to try to conserve energy.

I don't believe in fighting on the ropes. When you're against the ropes you're trapped. Getting out is almost always a problem, particularly with a smart fighter in front of you. When you feel the bottom strand hitting your calf, it's time to move laterally. As you're moving, throw jabs and combinations. Box your way back to the center of the ring.

COMBINATION PUNCHES

Whatever your style, you can't go wrong by becoming skillful in throwing combinations. Timing and technique are the keys to successful combination punching. Snap your punches without hesitation, and make certain that each part of the combination is a fundamentally sound punch.

If you're short, try to work inside your opponent's swings and attack the body.

When you're against the ropes, you're trapped. Getting out is almost always a problem, particularly with a smart fighter in front of you.

In the 1-2, as soon as the left jab lands, the straight right takes off. Merely shift the weight of your body to your right leg and let that side of your body swing forward with the punch.

In the 1-2-3, a left hook is launched the instant the straight right of a 1-2 hits the target. All you have to do is pivot on the ball of your left foot.

Observe that one punch flows from another. There is no need for abrupt changes in footwork or deviations from your normal techniques. Let your feet feel the rhythm and your fists supply the snap.

For the 1-3 combination, slide forward with your left foot; unleash the left jab; pivot on the ball of your left foot; and launch the left hook from short range. To make it a 1-3-2, transfer the weight to your right foot, immediately after the hook lands, and shoot out a straight right with your body behind it. Perhaps you wish to incorporate the uppercut into your combination. An ideal spot is immediately after a left jab.

Like the pool player who uses one shot to both sink a ball and set up another opportunity, you try to make each punch pave the way for the next. There are no hard and fast rules governing counterpunching sequences. Play it by ear; don't get overconfident; and do what comes naturally.

Timing and technique are the keys to successful counterpunching and combination punching. The fighter on the left (A) blocks a left with his right elbow; (B) counters with a left jab to the jaw; (C) follows with a right cross to the jaw; and (D) gets back into the basic position to catch a long left. Illustrations by Jill Koehl.

Southpaw Strategy 9

Tall or short, boxer or slugger, the lefthander comes equipped with a very valuable asset—the element of confusion. The southpaw is accustomed to clashing with righthanders. Consequently, his style is tailored to exploit the befuddlement of righthanded rivals. But there's no need to get messed up psychologically or be dismayed just because you're fighting a southpaw. He's actually easier to fight, scientifically, than a righthander.

Remember always to move to your left against the southpaw. By the same token, if you're lefthanded, try to force your opponent to go to his right.

Anticipate the lefty's moves and beat him to the punch. Lead with your right and use feints to set up openings for combinations with either hand. Use hooks and uppercuts with either hand.

For the lefthander, the most effective punches are the right hook, left cross, and left uppercut. Nevertheless, the southpaw who doesn't develop a right jab is making a big mistake. Many times the righthander will be wide open for the punch.

If you're a southpaw, the right jab will be a valuable punch should the time come when you're pitted against another lefty. He may be a sitting duck for your jab. But if you don't have one, and he does, you may turn into a clay pigeon.

All of the boxing techniques and fundamentals discussed in the earlier chapters are applicable to the lefthander. Let's review some of the essentials.

It is of the essence that the hands and feet work together to provide protection and power. Balance is the key to stance and movement.

Anticipate the lefthander's moves and beat him to the punch.

Slide to and fro without crossing your feet. Practice moving in all four directions. Lead with your right foot (if you're a lefty), and use your left for power and leverage. The first foot to move is the one closest to the position to which you are moving. Lateral movement and slipping will compound your opponent's confusion. Persistent punching will make it harder for him to adapt to your style. Don't be a head-hunter; the body is fair game, especially for your hook. Weight transfer and upper body movements are the same as those described in Chapters 4 and 5. The defensive fundamentals (Chapter 6) also are identical. Common sense demands that you learn to slip, catch, and brush punches. Counterpunching and putting together combinations are top priorities.

Because a lefthander is doing what comes naturally while a righthander is adapting, a southpaw boxing specialist will have a tendency to appear to be more skillful in the eyes of the judges. Therefore, a righthander

Uppercuts and hooks are effective punches against southpaws.

This lefthander has an excellent stance.

The lefthander should lead with his right foot and keep his left hand in position to protect his jaw.

The body is often open to a southpaw after he slips a right jab.

must take special precautions. Resist the temptation to throw an incessant barrage of straight rights, for you will be very vulnerable to a counterattack to the body, and you'll be stepping into the power alley of your opponent.

Use the right arm, elbow, and glove to block left hooks. Parry straight lefts, uppercuts, and right jabs with the right hand. If escape and evasion tactics are necessary, be sure to retreat to the left to avoid the southpaw's Sunday punch.

On offense against a southpaw, the left hook is an excellent weapon for a righthander to employ. A good move is a diagonal slide to the left, with a right hook to the body, followed by a left hook to the head. Another effective tactic is to throw a straight right to the head, then a left hook to the head or body.

Both right and lefthanders can profit from studying outstanding southpaw boxers. For the lefty, it will provide a means of incorporating new techniques into his fightplan and devising a stronger defense. For the righthander, the homework will come in mighty handy the next time he is tested by a southpaw. I repeat my earlier training tip: spar with a southpaw whenever you can.

Ring Psychology 10

Because amateur bouts are only three rounds in duration, the premium is on skill rather than slugging ability. The time is too short for you to rest your hopes on winning by knocking out your opponent.

Points are given for attack and defense. Attack includes clean and effective hits, aggressive action, and well-delivered partial hits. Points also may be deducted if you cover up with your hands so that your opponent is not in a position to hit.

Your best early strategy is to fight a defensive match with an offensive mental attitude. By that I mean tempting your opponent to take chances and then, when he exposes a weakness, capitalizing on the opportunity.

You must become proficient in defending yourself before attempting to become an offensive fighter. This is important both physically and psychologically. When a fighter fails in the ring, something is subtracted from his self-confidence. Early risks on your part increase the likelihood that you will make mistakes that will show up on the judges' scorecards. Later you'll have to play catch up.

In the ring the first two questions you should try to answer are, "What are my opponent's weaknesses? How can I pit my strengths against those weaknesses?" Is your jab keeping him at long range? When you go to the body what's his response? In brushing your punches does he sweep them to the outside or is he sloppy? Is he fooled by your feints? Are his movements and punches falling into a pattern? When you aren't fooled by his feints, does he throw the jab to keep you preoccupied?

Tall or short, you're operating on the

Lunging is poor offensive form and invites a counterattack. *Chicago Tribune* photo.

same principle. Work off your jab and off contact initiated by your opponent. Jab and slip. Jab and catch. Jab and block. Jab and brush.

Manipulate your opponent. Anticipate his moves; set him up; and make counter moves. Slip and counter. Catch and counter. Block and counter. Brush and counter.

After determining your adversary's fight-plan, work on disrupting it. Force him to play your game. For example, when an opponent is attempting to pressure you against the ropes, work side-to-side to keep him in the center of the ring.

If you can avoid it, never give your opponent an opening for his Sunday punch.

As the bout proceeds, keep an open mind. But never change a winning fight-plan. That is a cardinal rule. Countless triumphs have been turned into defeats because the fighter ahead on points in the final round got greedy and reckless and went for a KO against a slugger.

By the same token, if you have built your lead by being aggressive, don't start retreating and give your opponent the chance to win the third round in compelling fashion. It may cost you the fight.

Points will be deducted if you cover up with your hands so that your opponent is not in a position to hit.

You must become proficient at defense before attempting to become an offensive fighter.

Psychology and strategy are inseparable. In sizing up your opponent, don't permit him to psych you. His words and prefight antics are irrelevant. Your sole concern should be discovering his strengths and weaknesses and executing your strategy against them. The best psychological defense against a con artist is to pay no attention to his needling. By replying, you reveal that he has disrupted your concentration.

You need emotional drive to master boxing. But you also need emotional control. The ability to take a punch, for example, is in some degree related to a person's feeling about his ability to take a punch. A person who is fearful that he will be hurt, defeated, or knocked out is more easily hurt, defeated, or knocked out than a relaxed boxer who feels he can cope with anything that comes his way.

Catch and counter: after blocking a left hook, follow with a left uppercut.

Should your opponent take some cheap shots or hit below the belt, refrain from doing likewise. The referee may miss a foul the first time it happens, but if your opponent continues to fight dirty it will catch up with him. By trying to get even you run the risk of being the one who is penalized.

No matter how much your opponent enrages you by his words and actions, resist the temptation to start swinging in anger. To master boxing you must be a thinking man, not an angry man.

Always strive for perfected relaxation and control. This is the most important basic in boxing and, in my opinion, it applies to all sports and to everyday life, as well.

Professional Competition

Although the fundamentals of any sport remain the same regardless of the level of competition, the athlete must make psychological and physical adjustments when he advances from amateur to professional standing.

The contrasts between the pro fight game and amateur boxing are even more pronounced than the differences between high school basketball and the National Basketball Association. Success in amateur boxing suggests a promising pro career but doesn't guarantee it. Conversely, some outstanding pros were unable to win amateur titles.

Amateur fights generally place more of a premium on defensive dexterity. The winner of each round receives twenty points, the loser, nineteen or less. When points are equal, the edge goes to the boxer who did the most leading. Points are scored for blocking and avoiding punches as well as for landing them. A knockdown carries no more weight with the three judges than a jab to the head.

The referee uses three words of command:
—"Stop" to halt action
—"Box" to resume the fight
—"Break" to end a clinch (both contestants must step back before resuming).

It is a foul to hold with one hand and hit with the other, to punch backhand, or to wrestle with an opponent. After two warnings, the referee has the power to take a round away from a boxer who continually violates the rules.

When the referee believes a boxer still on his feet is unable to defend himself, he stops action and gives a standing eight-count to

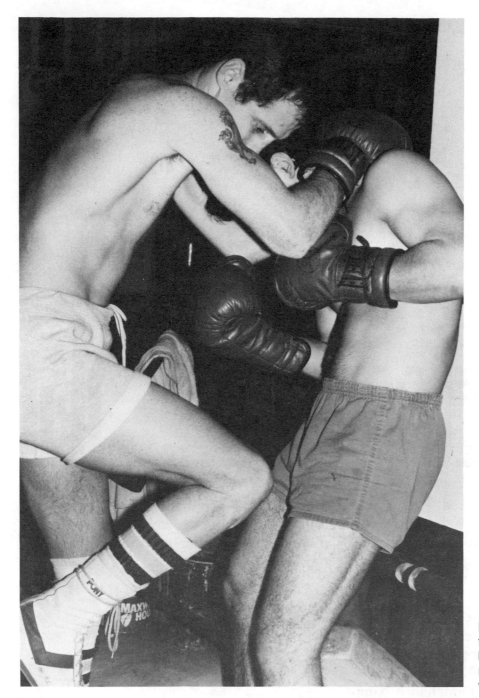

In amateur boxing, after two warnings the referee has the power to take a round away from a boxer who violates the rules.

enable the contestant to recover. As in the case of the conventional knockdown, blows which cause the standing knockdown don't collect a bonus on the scorecards. But amateur refs are quick to stop bouts that are becoming lopsided.

The standing knockdown is nonexistent in pro boxing, and referees are more reluc-tant to stop fights because the outcome has a bearing on the contestants' future income potential. It isn't uncommon to see a fighter who has been knocked down more than once, and taken an early battering, rally in the later rounds and emerge the winner.

While amateur bouts are all three rounds in duration, pro matches can be four, six,

Chuck Bodak gets former heavyweight champ Jimmy Ellis ready for a sparring session. Ellis was a Golden Gloves champion before turning professional. Elite Studio photo.

eight, ten, twelve, or fifteen rounds. Pace is tremendously important, since a contestant has a much longer time in which to achieve results from his strategy. For instance, a body attack that continues for seven rounds can turn a swifty into a man in slow-motion by round eight, and his entire defense may consequently topple.

Repeated blows to the head over several rounds may eventually batter a fighter into submission. Or a slugging specialist may not be able to tag his opponent with a knockout punch until late in the fight.

Because pro scoring is done by a referee (and two judges) who is close enough to the fighters to get a good view of infighting, a fighter skilled at infighting probably has a better chance of picking up points through his penetration.

Scoring varies from state to state. Most states use the ten-point system for each round, but some score by awarding whole rounds to one fighter. In the latter case, the extent of a fighter's domination is minimized. For example, in a ten-round match it's possible for you to give your opponent a tremendous beating for four rounds but have him win the fight by virtue of a slim advantage in the other six rounds. "Hometown decisions" are notorious in pro boxing on the club level.

I think it's vital for a boxer who wants to embark on a pro career to obtain as much experience as possible in the amateur ranks. I've seen far too many cases of fighters who turned pro too soon, only to have their confidence destroyed simply because their limited experience and immaturity didn't enable them to cope with their opponents and the pro environment.

Competition in the Golden Gloves, Amateur Athletic Union, and military service tournaments is recommended. Engagements against fighters from foreign countries are a tremendous prep for a pro career, and the best background of all is fighting in the Olympics and Pan-American Games.

In addition to a boxer's history, his geography and economics must be considered prior to the start of a pro career. Outside of California and New York, there is a shortage of pro fighters in the flyweight, bantamweight, and featherweight classes. To find competition and make some money, the newly turned pro from elsewhere in the nation probably will either have to relocate or run a gauntlet of one-night road stands.

Before turning professional you should talk it over with experienced and respected pro fighters. Be wary of the guy constantly pressuring you to sign a contract that makes him your manager. It's a good idea to discuss the proposed contract with the athletic director of your high school or with sportswriters whom you have gotten to know. They may recommend that you see a lawyer who will study the terms of the proposed contract (for a fee) to make certain that you're getting a square deal.

Pro boxing exerts heavier demands on both your time and talent. You must be truthful to yourself in evaluating your progress and potential. Continued improvement is a must if you are to make a living as a boxer. Set short-term and long-term goals. You must be motivated. Motivation means an intense desire to succeed in an occupation that demands a long-term commitment to sacrifice, bravery, and hard work.

Getting to the top and staying there requires an enormous amount of character. A scene from the movie *The Hustler* brings out my point. The pool-shark played by Paul Newman had great mental and physical gifts but lacked the discipline to keep success from going to his head. He was playing a game for high stakes against old Minnesota Fats (Jackie Gleason) and had a commanding lead. The more he won the higher he soared on his ego trip. But a betting man (George C. Scott) sized up the situation and wasn't fooled. "I'm going to keep betting on Minnesota Fats," the betting man whispered. "This other guy is a born loser—he's all skill and no character."

Mastering boxing builds both a strong body and a strong character. Most important, in striving to reach your goals you are also laying the foundation for a happy and successful life.

Index